A Fantastic Trip

Written by Tony Bradman
Illustrated by Beatriz Castro

Collins

It was three in the morning, but Scarlet was not asleep.

She put on her dressing gown and crept downstairs to get a drink.

Dad was snoring upstairs. Scarlet grabbed a carton of milk and turned to go back to bed. But then she got a fright!

What is that?

A bright light filled the garden.
Scarlet grabbed the broom and went to look.

As soon as she stepped out, the light scooped her up into the air ...

... and sucked her into a starship! A little green blob stood next to Scarlet. It seemed glad to see her.

Greetings. I'm Scarlet.

The blob handed her a spoon and pointed to a jar.

Bloop bloop bop!

Do I need to feed you?

7

The blob slurped its dinner off the spoon.

Then it grabbed a map and jumped on Scarlet's lap. But Scarlet did not understand.

Bloop bop bleep!

The blob frowned. Then it started to screech!

It ran to the corner and pressed a big red button.

Bright red sparks spurted from the boosters. The starship zoomed off, speeding by the moon. It swooshed on and on.

Look out!

All of a sudden, the starship screeched to a stop.

Stardust filled the air.

A big blob with green fluff floated in.

It scooped the little blob into its arms. The little blob blushed.

In her green dressing gown, Scarlet looked like the twin of the big blob.

14

The little blob had mixed up Scarlet with its mum!

The starship dropped Scarlet back in her garden.

"I will never forget that trip!"

The next morning, Scarlet's dad was complaining downstairs.

The broom is missing!

17

Planet map

Scarlet's planet

Moon

Mars

comet

Blob Planet

starship

Saturn

19

Blob Planet

A fantastic trip

23

🐾 Review: After reading 🐾

Use your assessment from hearing the children read to choose any words or tricky words that need additional practice.

Read 1: Decoding
- On pages 10 and 11, ask the children to look for these words and explain them in context:

  frowned (e.g. *made a face to show it was unhappy*)

  spurted (e.g. *suddenly shot out*)

- Challenge the children to blend in their head when they read these words:

asleep	**jumped**	**swooshed**
crept	**grabbed**	**dressing**

Read 2: Prosody
- Turn to pages 2 and 3. Focus on the punctuation and how it guides the reader to read with expression.
  - Point to the comma on page 2 and explain that it makes the reader pause. Encourage the children to read page 2, pausing at the comma. Point out how the comma causes an emphasis on **but.**
  - Point out the exclamation mark on page 3. Ask: What feelings can you put into this sentence? Check they notice the question mark in the speech bubble and use a questioning tone, too.
  - Encourage the children to reread the pages.

Read 3: Comprehension
- Ask the children to describe any other favourite stories they have read or seen that include an alien or starship.
- Reread pages 12 and 13, and discuss why the blob blushed. (e.g. *it was embarrassed that it mixed up who its mum was*) Ask: Do you think Scarlet would have had this fantastic trip if the blob hadn't made a mistake? Why? (e.g. *no because the blob would have scooped up its mum instead*)
- Bonus content: Ask the children to make up their own story about the little blob, using the pictures on pages 20 and 21.
- Turn to pages 22 and 23. Ask the children to retell the story, using the pictures as prompts.